# Measure for Living

# Measure for Living

Devotions and
Poems of Affirmation
by Roy Z. Kemp

Designed and illustrated
by Gordon Brown

Published by
The C. R. Gibson Company
Norwalk, Connecticut

# Dedication

For My Mother

Ethel Laura Nicholson Kemp

---


Printed in the United States of America
Library of Congress Catalogue Card Number: 67-29309

# Contents

# Preface

## *Christian Poetry*

Poetry moves on the higher levels of power and emotion, and it is the product of a maker of ideas. The truly creative artist of the written word is gifted with the ability to take the common facts and experiences of life and invest them with epic and enduring qualities.

The heart and core of inspirational poetry is a spirit of reverence and devotion. It is idealistic in nature, spiritual in quality, moral at its center, and is endowed with a richness of joy, of fellowship, of understanding and of the constantly fresh discovery of the eternal secret of friendship with God.

The longing for companionship with God has the highest emotional appeal. It is man's greatest need. Man's hunger for God is as fundamental as is his natural hunger for food. It rises above all else.

A spiritually perceptive poet is one who realizes that man cannot always change external things. He realizes also that we must rise above those things which would pull us down.

A person must be made aware of and be confirmed in the belief that he is a member of a moral order, that God exists and is concerned with man, and that man must, in return, be concerned with his fellowmen as well as with himself. The poet helps him see this.

Good Christian — or inspirational — poetry must have a universal appeal. It must possess a sincerity of expression, a deepness of thought, a basic philosophy, true to the Bible, expressed in poetical cadence — all of which anyone and everyone should understand and comprehend.

God is not limited to any one nation or people, nor to any one age. Throughout the centuries He has never let Himself be without witnesses. The literature of religion is most comprehensive. The Christian's viewpoint differs from that of the non-Christian's, yet the eternal verities as expressed in the Bible remain the same throughout the ages.

Poetry is the natural language of beauty, worship and love. It is the type of writing which is most effective in expressing the universal feelings of faith in God and in the goodness of things.

Poetry is the language of the heart. The incentives of Christian poetry are to activate and to cultivate Christian principles. Inspirational poetry fosters religious insight, offers guidance and counseling of a spiritual nature, and develops a sense of the sacred within every reader.

In our need for inner peace of mind and soul, we people of today seem to look everywhere except to God, the author of peace. Our age vainly searches for peace of mind and body, for peace of soul. But the blessings of God are not promised merely to the possessor of peace, but to the sharer of peace.

And this is what the writer of inspirational poetry is doing when he presents his work to his reader. In his own way, he is sharing peace and trying to produce some pleasure, inspiration and enjoyment for others.

# Faith

" . . . the just shall live by his faith."

Habakkuk 2:4

# Faith

Faith is not some vague and hazy quality which one is supposed to have in times of stress, acquired by some sudden means, in an unknown manner, — a thing which is abstract, formless, remote. Faith is, instead, the working of God's Spirit within us, "the substance of things hoped for, the evidence of things not seen." (Hebrews 11:1).

Faith is that quality within us which enables us to reach out into the unknown and grasp the unseen hand of God.

In John 4:24, Jesus says: "God is a Spirit: and they that worship him must worship him in spirit and in truth." It is essential to every man's happiness that he know the true God of the Bible, Father, Son and Holy Spirit. To many millions of persons, God is unreal, mystical and vague, whom they feel they cannot know intimately.

Yet it is in this God that every human being lives, moves and has his being. God holds the world in the palm of His hands. God is eternal. God is of the past, the present and the future. He was, He is and He shall always be. (Revelation 1:8).

A Christian's faith is focused upon Jesus Christ, our Lord and Saviour, the Christ of the manger, the cross, the empty tomb, the only Son of God; Christ, He who makes us just, righteous, and as newborn sons of God also.

In John 14:9, Jesus tells us that He and the Father are one. Hebrews 13:8 tells us that Jesus Christ is the same yesterday and today and forever.

God is the source of all life. His reign is supreme. He is the Light which banishes all darkness, the Great

Physician who heals all sickness of sin. And He is no respecter of persons. All of us are equal in His sight. It is through faith in Him that we live and have our hope.

Faith is a gift of God and a trust in His revealed Word. It is not a bare knowledge but rather a confidence of the heart in things we have accepted as truth. (Romans 10:10 and Heb. 11:1) Faith is the assurance and trust in spiritual things which we cannot see but which are promised to us by God in His Word, particularly in the Gospel message.

Yet — faith without works is dead! All who are filled with faith will in love be workers in the service of God. True faith is not of ourselves. It is the gift of God without any merit on our part. He who gave us faith will also preserve it for us. When we experience true peace, joy and happiness, this is not faith in itself, but rather a result of our faith.

Faith is a simple word, but often it is misused and misunderstood. Faith is simply believing and trusting in God's love and promises; faith is accepting Jesus as the Son of God and as our Lord and Saviour, trusting Him for forgiveness of our sins, for assurance of eternity with Him, for peace within ourselves. Without Christ, faith is nothing, for faith is looking to Jesus, depending upon Him, leaning on Him, clinging to Him.

How wonderful it would be if each and everyone of us could recapture the fiery faith of the first Disciples. While God is a spirit, man is both body and spirit. As a Christian, he must ask that the right spirit be renewed within him, and by so doing, he is drawn nearer and closer to God. He must lose himself to find himself. His old self of sin must die that he may become a new creature, redeemed by grace. In losing, he finds that he is saved; in dying, he finds that he lives.

## *We Must Have Faith*

We must have faith! We must believe
The Lord is on our side.
If this our hearts cannot accept,
His love shall not abide.
The Lord is merciful and kind;
His will is always done;
He soothes the troubled, heals the sick,
Aids each afflicted one.

We may not always understand
The reasons for His way
Nor always fully comprehend,
But we must each obey
And question not. Our faith and trust
Must never wane nor pale.
God knows our needs — He will provide,
And He will never fail.

## *Bright Morning*

I shall not fear the night,
For dawn will come
And dissipate the fright,
The mist, — the sum
Of all discordancy;
Then, I shall know
Heart's freedom and its glee.
All fear will go.

With darkness gone, shall go
Its darkened curse;
The glare of sun shall rule
My universe.
Life filled with laughter, joy,
My mind set free,
My burden light, a glad day
Waits for me!

### *A Christian's Faith*

A Christian's faith enables him
To take each day in stride,
To have the courage to accept
The loss of face and pride,
Good health or sickness, life or death,
Or happiness or sorrow,
Success or failure, — any thing
Brought by a new tomorrow.

A Christian has the stamina
That makes for deep belief,
It strengthens him in hours of doubt
And comforts him in grief;
It stands with him in hours of trial,
It clears the path he'll trod,
It gives him courage for the fight,
It brings him close to God.

### *If Faith Be Strong*

Sometimes we follow logic's path,
Sometimes our fancy leads
And we must chase will-o'-the-wisps
To satisfy our needs.

Sometimes our hearts are broken and
Sometimes our hearts are gay,
But, nonetheless, each one must go
Along his chosen way.

But if we go courageously
And walk by faith's strong light,
Our destination will be reached;
Each one will win his fight.

## *Moments*

One quick, short breath is what a moment is,
A tiny golden bit within an hour,
An infinitesimal space from dawn to dusk,
Yet it contains a magnitude of power.

Within a moment battles may be won,
Life may be given or life may depart;
It may contain great sorrow or great pleasure,
Or usher love into a lonely heart.

Our lives are lived one moment at a time
And no man knows what the next moment brings.
Look up with faith, continuing life's journey;
Like stars, our moments are most precious things!

## *In Touch with God*

Each day I am in touch with God.
    I feel His healing hand,
I hear His low and gentle voice
    And heed each sweet command.

I listen when He speaks to me.
    My path is straight and clear.
With spirit high, serene, and free,
    There is no bounded fear.

With heart completely filled with hope,
    My feet are lightly shod;
There is no problem I can't face —
    I am in touch with God.

## *Our Pilot*

Though billows roll
And waves be mountain high,
Be not afraid
For our dear Lord is nigh.
Hold to His hand
And pray on bended knee;
Our faith and trust
Will help to calm the sea.

Be not alarmed,
Pull steady on the oars;
Hold to the course,
Heed not the ocean's roars.
Eventually
The sunshine will break through,
The storm will pass.
God stands along with you.

## *Belief*

I have no faith in destiny,
Do not believe in fate,
I do not think blind force should rule
Nor men who rant and prate.

I think the world is better now
Than it was yesterday,
And I believe tomorrow will
Be better than today.

I think whatever rock may lie
Within the road I trod
Is placed there for a stepping stone,
For I believe in God.

## *O Light of Ages*

O Light of Ages, shine into each mind
And let each soul a lighted pathway find.

Show each the truth and make his faith secure;
Give him the strength and courage to endure.

Rekindle spirit; let Thy love proclaim
The blessed radiance of Thy dear name.

Hold Thou his hand and lead him to the Way,
To the eternal light of perfect day.

## *Saviour*

I could not find my way.
    There was no star
To guide me down the roadway,
    Rugged, far;
I had believed someone
    Would welcome me,
Would blaze a trail, leave signs
    For me to see.

So, lost, alone, I floundered
    In the dark,
Trod a strange path, bewildered
    As a lark
With broken wing. God heard
    My cry of pain;
He spoke and smiled . . . My world
    Was right again!

## *Consolation*

If your heart be filled with courage,
  If your soul be filled with prayer,
God will give you strength for working
  But not make your roadway fair.

Through the trials that He gives you,
  Through the hardship's hurts and stings,
God is measuring and shaping
  You for better, greater things.

## *Millennium*

They are not free,
Those fearful ones who are content to dwell
In darkness, in defeat; who cannot see
That dawn will soon appear, and all is well.

When eyes are dim,
The visions of new heaven and new earth
Cannot be seen; the glorious new hymn
Cannot be heard by ears long dead to mirth.

The free shall know,
Those fearless and courageous men who stand
Undaunted, unafraid before the foe
That stealthily advances through the land.

Soon peace will come,
Fear will be shattered, and uncertainty
Dispelled, the force of evil will be numb,
And faith will live again, doubt cease to be.

# Hope

"Turn you to the stronghold, ye prisoners of hope."

Zechariah 9:12

# Hope

Hope is the quality within our hearts which enables us to continue going. It is the thing which gives meaning and direction to our lives. The hope of glory — an eternal hope — is the aim and goal of every living soul, obtained only through faith in our Redeemer and Saviour, Jesus Christ.

Hope is the anchor of the soul, both sure and steadfast, as we are told in Hebrews 6:19. It is firmly anchored within the being of every Christian and sustains him through every adversity. Romans 8:24 tells us that "we are saved by hope."

Hope is a vital and living thing or it is nothing at all. Without hope, life may be compared with dead ashes; but with a vibrant hope in our heart, life is a magnificent triumph, for in hope lies our belief in His resurrection and of our life with Him in eternity.

A Christian has hope that is sure and steadfast. Nothing is able to deter or destroy this hope. It seems unthinkable that we can even live without hope, without a belief in a better life to come. We may hope for better health for ourselves and our loved ones, for a better world, for our own success and advancement in our work, but the greatest hope is our hope for eternity.

Hope can make each of us become a better person. Hope can dispel loneliness and heartache, weariness and frustration. Hope can revive and invigorate; it can beget joy; it can annihilate despair. Hope is made up of expectation, patience, fortitude, understanding, and belief. Hope is a characteristic of the Christian.

Hope is a virtue and can in no way be identified with shallow optimism or temporary cheerfulness. Hope requires the discipline of both thought and prayer, a steadiness of mind and will. Hope is an important thing; it is most influential in our lives. Hope can enable us to continue the daily hard struggle for existence.

That man whose hope does not reach beyond the grave or beyond the boundaries of this world is wretched indeed. Despair is his only prospect. In Ephesians 2:12 St. Paul has written a tragic epitaph for such unbelievers, those without hope: "Having no hope, and without God in the world."

There is no better nor blessed bondage than to be a prisoner of hope.

## *Who May Hope*

Who may hope to share a sorrow
Who has never had to grieve?
Who may hope for joys of friendship
Who has practiced to deceive?

Who may hope to feel compassion
Who has never understood?
Who may hope for faith or mercy,
Knowing not man's brotherhood?

He who lives within himself
Never tastes of great applause.
All his victory's fruit is bitter
And he fights an empty cause.

## *Certainty*

Though evil seem triumphant now, and men
Afraid and weak of heart, I know that He
Has not forgotten us or gone away.
He was, He is and shall forever be!

## *Dawn of Hope*

The darkness of despair is deep,
For when the spirit's desolate,
Illusions shattered, faith asleep,
The bitterness of grief is great.

But when the dawn of hope awakes,
All coward souls new courage find,
For radiant morning glory breaks
The bonds of fear, the doubts of mind.

## Hope

Hope is not a frail thing,
But one good and strong;
Hope can give you courage
When everything goes wrong.

Hope can be a cheerful friend,
Hope can bring you peace;
Hope can conquer terror,
Cause all your fears to cease.

Hope was made for everyone,
So hope is never odd;
Hope brings great delight
For hope comes straight from God.

## The Resurrection

If Death has not the power
To keep within its grasp
The tiniest and smallest seed,
But lets it sprout and clasp
The warm embrace of rain and sun,
To grow and blossom white,
How could Death ever hope to hold
The One who is the Light?

How could Death ever hope to hold
Within a cold, dark tomb,
To keep Him hidden and unseen
Until the day of doom
The One whose heart was made to live?
Death was a fool, not clever,
That day it sought to keep its own
The One who lives forever!

## *Free Spirit*

Those bowed in grief or cowed by fear
Must live in darkness, year by year.
But those who know joy, great and bright,
Shall not be filled with pain of fright.

A wholesomeness pervades the soul,
Each spirit shall be free and whole,
For gaiety will rend asunder
The morbid pangs of grief's dark thunder.

## *When Hearts Are Glad*

Who walks along with sorrow,
    Will travel bitter roads;
Will carry heavy burdens
    And bear most heavy loads.

Who walks with joy and gladness,
    Will dance along the street,
Because the happy heart
    Will make for nimble feet.

## *Changes*

Where laughter is,
    There has been pain;
Where sunshine is,
    There has been rain.

All yesterdays
    Were once tomorrows,
And, surely, joys
    Will follow sorrows.

## *Tomorrow — Gladness*

Tomorrow, there shall be for me
    Sunshine and clouds of blue,
Though now a gray and misty sky
    Obliterates my view.

Tomorrow, I shall surely find
    Great happiness indeed,
But for today the sorrows cling
    And I am filled with need.

Tomorrow, a new day dawns,
    A great awakening
Shall come, my heart so filled with joy,
    Enraptured will I sing!

## *In Praise of New Things*

Serenity is found in common things
And peacefulness in methods known by rote.
The strange, unusual may bring concern,
May bring disquietness, the worried note.

Yet, newness must be tried, for there we find
A piquancy, a flavor all its own.
Tranquility may thrive on common things,
But knowledge comes from testing the unknown.

# Charity

"By love serve one another."

Galatians 5:13

# Charity

"Though I speak with the tongues of men and of angels, and have not charity, I am become as sounding brass, or a tinkling cymbal. And though I have the gift of prophecy, and understand all mysteries, and all knowledge; and though I have all faith, so that I could remove mountains, and have not charity, I am nothing. And though I bestow all my goods to feed the poor, and though I give my body to be burned, and have not charity, it profiteth me nothing." (1 Corinthians 13:1-3)

In our present day usage of the English language we would undoubtedly substitute the word "love" for the word "charity" to better express the thought of the above passage. In this day and age there is a desperate need for love. While we were created for love, we live in an age where there is an acute absence of love brought about to a large extent by the depersonalized and organized functioning of our society. To a degree this situation already existed in Bible times. St. Paul in the third chapter of his letter to Titus calls attention to man's foolishness, disobedience, malice, envy and hate for one another, but then goes on to point out that in spite of all this, the love of God our Saviour still appears to mankind and that in mercy He saves us.

Service of love, performed in the name of our blessed Lord and Saviour, will not go unrewarded. The Lord has promised in grace to reward the faithful deeds of love performed by those who love Him. God's children should consider it a glorious privilege to assist others faced with the many and varied problems of life. Our concern must come because of our love for and our faith in God and His blessed Son our Saviour.

A living faith is always active in good works and as we have been instructed, the greatest of these is charity or love. In this connection we should always remember that God wants us to use our talents, our services and our possessions for the welfare of others and for the greater building of His Kingdom. Giving of ourselves and our possessions is part of God's plan for our salvation. God's greatest gift was the giving of His Son in love for all of mankind.

God cheerfully gives to each of His children every moment of every day. He richly and daily provides us with all of our bodily needs. He defends us against danger, guards and protects us from evil. All this He does out of fatherly goodness and mercy, without any merit or worthiness on our part. We are as sponges, greedily soaking up both spiritual and physical blessings. It is, however, His will that we share our blessings rather than to withhold them for our own enjoyment and use.

## *Acts of Service*

The tiny crumbs of joy and happiness
That we may scatter all along our way,
May seem quite insignificant to us,
But we may bring a bright and golden ray
Into the lives of some unfortunate,
Unhappy souls who trod hard weary roads;
Each little crumb may be a lavish feast,
Give sustenance to lighten heavy loads.

One crumb may be a gentle, friendly smile;
Another, just a letter to a friend;
A tiny kindness to a little child;
A helping hand to one who's reached the end.
Such little things that may not stay in mind
For very long, may be great things, indeed.
God, grant that we retain the wisdom to
Give aid and succor to someone in need.

## *For One Troubled*

Whatever hurts us, hurts our Father more.
The deepest places of His heart
Are filled with love, compassion; pity, too,
To know that pain and grief must play a part
In helping each of us to understand
That grief and sorrow are a part of life.
Souls must anvil-tempered be for strength,
Withstand vicissitudes and every strife.

We must not question why, must not complain
About our heavy burdens, troubles, woes.
Our Father knows each one, and He will send
The strength which we will need. So well, He knows
Our needs! If we but trust Him as we should,
In His own time all things work toward our good.

## *Prayer for Charity*

Let me forget the unkind word
Which someone says to me,
Remembering the kind and good
Is all that there should be
Within my mind. The hurt, the blow,
And humiliation's sting
Must be forgotten just as though
There had not been a thing.

And let my own mistakes and faults,
Or any unkind word
I may have done or may have said
When I was quick and stirred,
Be soon forgotten by the ones
Who may have heard or seen.
Be charitable of all these things,
Dear Lord, and make me clean!

## *Prayer for a Generous Heart*

I have received so many gifts,
Dear Lord, from Thy abundant store,
How can I not be satisfied?
How dare I ask for one thing more?

I sing a song of thankfulness,
For I've received so very much,
Yet teach me how to share Thy love
With everyone whose life I touch.

# Praise

"O sing unto the Lord a new song:
sing unto the Lord, all the earth."

Psalm 96:1

# Praise

The only lasting glory is God's glory. This is the eternal splendor. Glory signifies splendor, great renown, magnificence, and these things call forth admiration and praise.

The glory of God is portrayed in the anguish of the Cross, where His blessed Son suffered and died so that we might be forgiven our sins and thus be redeemed by His blood. When we are confronted by the saving message of the Gospel, we glorify God by singing, "Glory be to the Father and to the Son and to the Holy Ghost; as it was in the beginning, is now and ever shall be, world without end."

Man-given praise and glory usually is fleeting and transitory. It contains no lasting quality, for man is always looking for another person to idolize, to glamorize. In any contest or competition, the victor or winner is remembered — but only so long as he continues to win. A loser is quickly forgotten and placed in obscurity's niche.

In our daily lives, it sometimes appears that our worries and sorrows hide God from our sight. As a result we tend to fall into the pit of despair. But, as Christians, we should realize that God, although unseen, is always very close to us. We must retain the assurance that His grace is shining upon us, that He is always ready to help us by the presence and power of His Holy Spirit.

God has never promised His followers that they would be entirely free from vexing problems, but He has told us that He will be with us in our trouble. (Psalm 91:15)

We are never able to discover the glory of God by ourselves. God must enlighten our hearts and minds and bring us to a saving knowledge of His person and His work. We must, therefore, throw ourselves upon His mercy, acknowledge that He has full power over us and ask for His grace. There is never a day in our lives when we do not need the mercy of the Lord.

## *Spirit of Glory*

Love is a spirit of glory
That dwells within the heart
And where it lives, lives honor
And grace and truth in part.
No bargaining will gain it,
No pleas, no sacrifice;
It comes without a warning,
Without a tag of price.

Its stature grows more splendid
And finer and more tall;
The more that it is given,
The more it will enthrall.
So wonderful a treasure,
Yet any heart may hold
Its golden, shining splendor
To guard against the cold.

## *Surety*

Who seeks to find the love of God,
Need only ask. His loving arm
Will draw you close in warm embrace
And keep you safe from fear and harm.

But he who flees the wrath of God
And would escape His angry face,
Will find there is no place to run;
Will find there is no hiding place.

## *"Glory"*

"Glory" signifies magnificence.
It calls for admiration and for praise.
Men may achieve a certain radiance,
Receive an adulation many ways,
But transitory is this recognition;
There is no permanency in this condition.

The only lasting glory is God's glory,
For here is splendor that shall be eternal.
Our God, alone, is wise. It is His story
That brings a saving knowledge. This, the kernel
Of saving truth. And God we glorify
With all our love, our life, — or else we die.

## *Our Saviour*

He is a listener to those who pray,
He is a comforter to those who weep,
He's the forgiver to the ones who sin,
If they but ask, if they His word will keep.

He's a provider for the ones in want,
He gives His blessings to the ones in need,
He's a sustainer to the ones who toil
And every hungry soul he'll gladly feed.

He is our Friend, our hope and our salvation.
How wonderful and joyous this is so.
He says He is the Way, the Truth, the Life;
No greater knowledge can we ever know.

## *The Second Feast*

The birds flew down that glorious day
When all the crowd had gone away,
To peck and eat the crumbs that lay
    So plentiful.

First, one flew down and then another,
Then each one flew to tell his mother,
His father, sister and his brother
    Of the bountiful.

They ate their fill of fish and bread
And every hungry bird was fed,
And many thankful prayers were said
    For the miracle.

## *Time*

There is a time, there is a place
    For things which we must do:
A time to weep when grief we feel,
    A time for gladness, too.

There is a time for gaiety
    And happiness and bliss,
But when a sorrow comes our way,
    There must be time for this.

There is a time to rest ourselves,
    A time to till the sod,
But we must make a greater time —
    The time to spend with God.

## *Those Who Would See*

He stood erect, but at a loss
Because he could not see.
The only way to view the cross
Is on a bended knee.

## *Silent Praise*

His stars are hushed, His hills are mute,
And still is His green sod,
And yet, with what great eloquence
They speak their love of God.

You need not shout your faith and praise;
A calm and peaceful heart
And trustful eyes and willing hands
May do a Christian's part.

## *Hunger*

Man's spirit hungers, feels the need
Of living truth on which to feed,
And man cannot be satisfied
Until this need is gratified.

And with this hunger in his heart,
Man cannot walk from God apart,
Nor would he nibble on a stone.
Man does not live by bread alone.

# Peace

"Peace I leave with you, my peace I give unto you."

John 14:27

# Peace

Peace is of divine origin; thus, it is completely satisfying and filling. It is strengthening to both mind and body. Divine peace fills us with grace. It comforts, protects and guards. It is a wellspring within our being, flooding and filling our souls with courage, hope and confidence. It annihilates restlessness, insecurity, fear and doubt.

The peace which the world gives holds no promise of eternity, nor does it answer our needs or satisfy our innermost unrest and dissatisfaction. Search as we may, we will always find that the world's peace is neither lasting nor satisfying. Such feelings of peace are transitory. The world cannot give genuine peace because it has none to give. Peace, we are told, is not of earthly manufacture.

We take Christ into our hearts by faith. Our soul's salvation is assured by faith in Christ Jesus, God's own Word of Peace. Philippians 4:7 informs us that the peace of God, which passeth all understanding, shall keep our hearts and minds through Christ Jesus.

For generations, in his search for inner peace, man has turned to the Bible. The things which men live by have their source in this great book, the Word of God. In its pages men have found light for their darkest hour, help for their greatest need, comfort for their shattered spirit.

The greatest deeds of courage and most sublime actions of men have been inspired by the Bible. Martyrs have dedicated their lives to its principles and have died with its words on their lips. In the Bible will be found that sublime flame which lifts all men's hearts, giving them inward peace, greater hope, stronger faith. It restores courage, lifts the spirit and teaches lessons of mercy, compassion, charity, tolerance.

To obtain true peace of mind, body and soul, it is necessary to have faith in the religion of the Bible based on salvation in Christ as expressed in the Gospels. As we enter the house of the Lord where His Word is taught, we are brought together with Him and the communion of saints. It is here, more than in any other place, that we behold the beauties of His grace. His church thus becomes a real haven of peace and comfort.

## *Aspiration*

I think that I would like to fly
On silver wings across the sky.

Bird-free, I know it would be grand
To wing my way above the land,

To sail above both land and sea
Into the blue infinity.

In His great peaceful atmosphere,
I would feel safe and have no fear,

Up there, far, far above the sod,
Up near the stars, up nearer God.

## *On Being Blind*

I cannot see the sun
From its high place,
But I can feel its presence
On my face.
I cannot see the clouds
That float on high,
Nor see their haunting shadows
Passing by.
I cannot hear your voice,
Now you are gone
Beyond the far gray reaches
Of the dawn,
But memory recalls
These things — so dear! —
And I can sense their presence
Ever near.

## *Jericho Road*

The stony road to Jericho —
O bitterest of roads! —
Its travellers are weary ones
Who carry heavy loads.

They start the journey eagerly,
With heaven in their eyes,
But many fall beside the way;
None hear their helpless cries.

But some may journey to the end —
These are the staunchest men —
They will see the smiling welcome
Of the Good Samaritan.

## *Unfathomable*

Our God, the great Creator,
Upon His throne of thrones,
Must like to see good order
Within the world He owns.

The harvest follows seedtime,
The sunshine follows rain,
The dawn comes after darkness,
And gladness follows pain.

And He must feel great sadness
To view this world below,
To see the fights and frictions,
To see our grief and woe,

He sees such great disorder . . .
I sometimes wonder why
He does not draw the curtains
And shut out earth from sky!

## *Measure for Living*

He who only walks in sunshine
Misses all the joy of rain;
He who never suffers hardship,
Must forego its healing pain.

To attain a perfect balance
And a rich, full life to live,
There must be a careful blending
Of all things which life can give.

## *Conscience*

Oh, may that small celestial light
Within each person's heart
Not flicker, wane, nor ever dim,
But play its beacon part.

Its small but steady flame is known
To commoners and kings;
It is a torch to light the way
To better, greater things.

## *Who Would Talk with God*

Who shouts to God in boisterous tone,
In loud and shrill accusing word,
Shall be as one alone and lost;
His brassy voice shall not be heard.

But he who speaks in gentle tone,
In prayer, with grateful heart and full,
Will find God's wise and lenient ear
Attuned to every syllable.

## *Still to Come*

Has mankind halted in his growth?
Are all experiments complete?
Are there no new horizons now?
Is man's work through, his leisure sweet?

The greatest song is still unheard,
The best of stories not yet told,
The finest poem still awaits
Creation in some poet's mold.

New strides in medicine are made
Each day to lessen pains and sorrows:
Men of science still provide
New ways and means for new tomorrows.

## *God's Testing*

Somehow, the darkest night will have an end
And morning, bright and fresh, shall surely dawn.
Have patience, trust and hope, and God will send
His blessed healing, bid despair be gone.

Look up with faith and wait this blessed healing.
He soon will gently wipe away your tears.
The little pricks of sorrow you are feeling
Are just God's way to test you down the years.

# Service

"The Lord our God will we serve, and his voice will we obey."

Joshua 24:24

# Service

All of us sense the need for purpose and direction in our lives. Yet conflicts of interest can become great pitfalls for many a Christian. He wants to be a disciple of Jesus, but not completely. He wants to be pure and holy and good, but not just yet. He wants to listen to God's voice, but not too much nor too often.

These are the feelings of separation, apartness and vacillation. Where God is concerned, there can be no conflict of interest. You must either choose to serve God or Mammon; you cannot do both.

Once we come to a realization of our relationship with Christ Jesus, we completely forget self. Our life will have purpose and direction, for when God calls and receives, there is power and blessing in abundance. We will be completely filled with the desire to serve.

One of the greatest of our tragedies is the lack of personal concern for our fellowmen. Prayer reveals concern and concern will always beget prayer. There are, of course, many concerns in our daily lives. But our greatest concern should be for people — all people.

We must first be concerned about people if we are to help them. Our concern must be unselfish. It must include both their bodily and spiritual welfare. We must have faith that God through His Spirit is working within those we are attempting to serve.

Our motivation for Christian service must be one of love and giving of self in thankfulness for God's great love and concern for each one of us. This is expressed in 1 John 4:11, which reads, "If God so loved us, we ought also to love one another." He, in love, gave His only Son to become man, to suffer and to die for all mankind.

The truly dedicated Christian is also a happy Christian. He surrenders himself completely to Christ and does not count personal loss or cost, but sees only the results. He is able to see men not for what they are, but for what they become and then in love puts forth every effort to this end.

On this basis we should utilize every opportunity to show our thankfulness in response to the indebtedness we owe our heavenly Father because of His great love for us. In living a life of unselfish service our spiritual life will, as a result, be enriched many fold.

## *Doing God's Work*

Now is the time for action and for deed.
Let us not stumble blindly, darkly grope,
But hold our candle high and let its flame
Provide a guiding light for comfort, hope.

Begin! And seize your opportunities.
There are so many things that we must do:
Give aid and succor, banish loneliness,
And bring to weary hearts strength fresh and new.

And let them know, those sickened with distress,
That other folk still feel and love and care.
Today, begin His work, and He will know
And will receive your good work as a prayer.

## *Shepherd*

There is no one more tender than a shepherd
No one more kind, more loving, full of grace;
No one more filled with Christ-like qualities,
Which show throughout his being, in his face.

He tends his flock with patient understanding
From break of dawn till setting of the sun;
He speaks with love, with gentle admonition,
And guards from harm each straying little one.

This man, who is so much a part of nature,
Is least contaminated with its sin,
He follows in the footsteps of the Master;
O worthy is this humble man or men!

### *Miracle Worker*

The one who helps a little child
To walk the way of truth
And guides its life, erasing all
That's evil, crude, uncouth,
Performs a modern miracle.
His work is good and sound.
In doing this God-given task,
He walks on hallowed ground.

### *Wise Planter*

Shared memories of boyhood days
Placed in a small boy's heart
By his wise father, soon will sprout;
They will become a part
Of all his hopes and plans and dreams.
The son will emulate
His loving parent. Wise the man
Who tills in soil so great.

### *Wish for Service*

Just let me be a candle
That God has set below,
To give a little added light
On roads that others go.
Oh, may my weak and tiny flame —
My faint and feeble spark —
Help light the pathway of someone
Who stumbles in the dark!

## *For Service Rendered*

The one who feels his labor lost
Unless he gets a great return
For all his effort, soon shall learn
How fruitless was his time, the cost.

No benefit will be derived
By anyone — and less by him;
If any gain, it will be slim,
And he the most dissatisfied.

But he whose work is freely given,
Whose body, spirit, soul and mind
Are used to help another find
Some knowledge, shall be blessed in heaven.

## *Little Acts of Service*

Each small and tiny candle's gleam
Can send a little light
Into a portion of the dark,
Into the blackest night.

The tiny ray may be the beam
Some lost soul needs, to guide
Him on the pathway home again,
Where loved ones wait with pride.

Each little friendly gesture made,
Each act of goodness done,
Is but a part of God's great plan
To help some needful one.

## *Possibilities*

One fragile word —
A friendship may be made,
Or courage given
To one who is afraid.

A single thought —
Life's lesson may be learned,
Decisions made
Where two roads have turned.

A little act —
Great mercy may be shown,
Shame turn to joy,
Fame come to one unknown.

## *Lights*

Faith is the light that dispels
 the power of darkness,
Hope is the light that brings closeness
 to ones far apart,
Trust is the light that hinders
 the growing of doubt,
Love is the light that illumines
 the way to each heart.

Friends are the lights which erase
 the power of strangeness,
Children are lights which make our lives
 cheerful and bright,
Parents are lights which complete
 and prepare us for living,
But Jesus, our Saviour, is greatest —
 our sweet guiding Light.

# Vision

"I will lift up mine eyes unto the hills,
from whence cometh my help."

Psalm 121:1

# Vision

Life without vision can be most dull and drab.
Each of us must have vision. We must have dreams: vision for a greater and better tomorrow and dreams for a brighter and more glorious future.

The means of obtaining vision and dreams, is to have a stronger faith, feel a purer love, live a better life, know a greater zeal for God's work, and be a more courageous witness for God.

Nothing must blur this vision; its brightness must never be dimmed nor its focus distorted. Nothing must ever kill our dreams. To be without vision and dreams, is to be dead. And many are the things which will attempt to change our vision, cloud our eyes, fog our minds.

But with God's help, our vision will remain eternally bright, our dreams continue to grow. As we find our fellowship in Him, we shall walk safely and surely toward the shining goal.

### *When Vision Comes*

I'm filled with doubt, uncertainty,
My heart is filled with dread
Whenever I can't know or see
The road which lies ahead.

But joy possesses heart and mind
And takes away the pain
When vision comes and I can find
The goal I must attain.

### *Eyes of Heart and Mind*

They who deny their living God
And yield to Satan's evil plea,
Are blind in heart and soul and mind,
Though having eyes with which to see.

Eyes only see material things,
But heart and mind are spirit lead
They reach the depths of hell's dark pit
Or climb the peaks that loom ahead.

### *Hearts*

When hearts are strong, they will not break
But beat away intruding ache.
And wise are hearts with love to hold
And guard against the bitter cold.

But hearts so spiritless and weak
That make all things to them look bleak,
Are foolish hearts that beg or borrow
Protection from a sad tomorrow.

## *Faith's Vision*

Our faith must be a living force
Within the heart and soul and mind,
Else it will be a deadened thing
And useless, we will always find.

But vitally alive, our faith
Will soar triumphantly on wings
Of living glory; joyous hymns
Of glory are the songs faith sings.

## *Holy Guardian*

The Lord is kind and He will give
    New vision to your eyes,
Instill your heart with confidence,
    Give wisdom to your mind;
If you will follow His command,
    The Master of the skies
Will lead you safely through the ways
    That evil has designed.

The Lord will still the storm of fear
    And give to you new peace,
He'll take away your weariness
    And give to you new rest;
The Lord is just and merciful,
    His love shall never cease
And if you'll show your love for Him,
    You will be doubly blest.

## *Shining Flame*

Great trust will live through deep distress
    And faith will live when ways are dark.
And courage lives with blessedness
    And gives to every heart a spark
Of glorious and added strength,
    A shining flame that's all its own,
With breadth and depth and width and length
    And greater than the heart had known.

So, knowing this, I shall have trust,
    And faith shall live within my soul;
Then courage shall remove the rust
    Of fear from heart and make me whole.
I need to know the shining flame
    Of courage sent from God on high;
To feel the love of His great name
    And know that it shall never die.

## *Vision*

The one who is content to rest at ease
Upon a self-acclaimed high pinnacle
Of some accomplishment, seeks not to please;
Achievement soon will tarnish and grow dull.

But he who strives to reach a higher goal,
Who perseveres, who seeks a greater glory,
Will know an honor; he will play a role
In some more splendid, finer, greater story.

## *The Wise Men*

Upon that night of glory long ago,
The wise men numbered three. They travelled far
With dauntless faith, with courage, and with hope
To find the Babe, led by His shining star.

Today, the wise men still are few, but these
Have kept their faith and courage. Each of them
Still has his hope; each trusting heart is warm;
Each follows still the Star of Bethlehem.

## *Points of View*

Though having sight, one could not see
Beauty of grass and leaf and tree.
The other, blind, could walk the earth
And know the beauteous spring's rebirth.

## *He Who Is a Light*

Whose heart is glad for one bright hour of beauty,
Who walks with faith, lifts up his life with prayer,
Who quickly moves to do his bidden duty
And who will graciously and gladly share,
Fulfills his mission and has grace to spare.

Who turns his days, his years, into a blessing,
Who marches on with courage in his eyes
When stormclouds threaten, when disaster's pressing,
Because he sees the light beyond dark skies,
Will be, himself, a light which never dies.

## *Hills*

God gave us hills for climbing
So each of us, each day,
May climb a little higher
And walk the upward way;
So we, with better vision,
May loose restraining bars
And leave our valley thinking
And follow hilltop stars.

## *A Bright Tomorrow*

Let us keep hope alive within our hearts.
Let not a single heart forget to pray.
Though sad may be our faces, spirits low,
We may look forward to another day.

God has a plan for every seeking pilgrim;
He has a peace for every heart that sorrows.
Though we may feel that discord lasts forever,
There will be harmony in our tomorrows.

Chaos persists in all the universe,
But calm fulfillment we shall each receive
If soul will hear the music of the spheres,
If heart has faith and hope and will believe.

# Small Things

"For who hath despised the day of small things?"

Zechariah 4:10

# Small Things

Great moments and exciting adventures come to very few of us. Life is made up of small, inconsequential things. And because small things usually are routine and trivial, we tend to come to regard them as being unimportant and humdrum. Many of us even chafe at them.

The quotation from Zechariah is a piercing question, one that each of us should ask ourselves. God holds us accountable also for the small things which go to make up our lives. Small things enter into God's judgment and can be the difference between a firm faith in our Lord and Saviour or one that wavers and as a result often spells the difference between having God's wonderful blessings bestowed upon us or from having them withheld.

Constant concern must be given to our great responsibilities. Good stewardship may well depend upon the care and faithfulness with which we discharge our responsibility in the small things we face in our day to day living.

There is a saying, "By remaining small and simple and unselfish, we may become something really big and important." We can do a great work of goodness or kindness. We can follow in the steps of the Lord, who "went about doing good," to the best of our ability, or perform the small tasks which have been appointed us in a manner which is gracious, kind, and competent.

The ark which carried the baby Moses was a tiny thing as it went sailing into the bulrushes with its most precious little cargo. The little fishes and the loaves of bread were also small, ordinary things, yet they became most precious and extraordinary in the hands of the Lord. The widow's mite, given from her generous heart, became a big thing in the eyes of the Lord.

Let us not despise the small or humble task. Often it is the small and apparently insignificant service which will represent our most valuable contribution to a worthy cause.

## *Little Boys*

Wonderful are little boys!
  They clutch you in an instant,
Though they are mostly made of noise,
  Their lives so far and distant.
And mostly they are impudent
  And saucy, brazen, bold,
But God was wisely provident —
  He gave them hearts of gold.

And boys are strange, mysterious,
  Yet open as a book;
They live a life nefarious
  With an angelic look.
And God must love all little boys,
  They fit into His plan;
They are the only things He'll use
  To make into a man!

## *Friends*

Good friendship is a miracle,
  It's sent from Him above
As proof of all His tender grace,
  As proof of all His love.

A friendly face, a friendly heart
  Are worth far more than gold,
For they are priceless in their worth,
  Their value can't be told.

A friend's a friend and friends are friends,
  I've found without regret;
I like to think all strangers are
  The friends I have not met.

## *Your Gift*

You may not have a shining coin to give,
  No royal purple robe to wear, no crown
Or diadem of gems, but few that live
  Possess these things, or even know renown.

Be not discouraged if your gift be small.
  Make up in service any lack in size.
A good name is the greatest gift of all,
  And loyal service shows you are most wise.

## *In Praise of Candles*

Things are lovelier at night
In a candle's golden light:
  Lovers sharing golden dreams,
  Building castles, planning schemes;
Children kneeling by their beds,
Praying little sleepy-heads;
  Dinner places at a table,
  Gowns of gingham or of sable —
It matters little, each may know
Great happiness in candle glow.

Candles are for daytime, too:
Birthday cakes, pink, white, or blue;
  They lend holiness and grace
  Lighting up an altar place.
Candles are most precious things!
They will cheer a heart that sings
  Or will lighten hearts grown sad,
  Helping banish all the bad.
With candlelight held in his hand,
One may walk safely through the land.

## *To Baby*

Soft little hands
That gently curl and clutch
Around my heart, how can you hold so much?

Wee, tiny things,
So tenderly you clasp,
Yet all my world lies in your little grasp.

Sweet mystery,
God-given bit of flesh,
My heart and soul you easily enmesh,

O Baby mine,
Within your gay, bright eyes,
I catch a glimpse of Heaven and paradise!

## *We Who Receive*

"Ask — and it shall be given;
Ask — and ye shall receive."
These promises are given us
Whose hearts always believe.

Generously God will bless us,
Who stand with hands upraised,
Whose hearts, when prayers are answered,
Are not one bit amazed.

But does God — sometimes — wonder
(Seeing hands lifted up,
Knowing the vastness of His stores),
At the smallness of our cup?

*Pygmy*

In his own puny intellect,
   Man sees far more of self
Then he can see of God, thus he,
   In stature, is an elf.

*Measurements*

When God grants us
The opportunity
To take the measurements
Of a man,
We put our tape
Around his waist for size
Of girth,
We measure arms for length,
Inseam to ankle
For the length of leg.

God does it differently.
He does not care
About the size of waist,
The length of leg or arm.
God only wants to know
One thing:
How really big the man is.
So, His tape is used to measure
Just one thing:
The heart.

# Prayer

" . . . Lord, teach us to pray."

St. Luke 11:1

# Prayer

Prayer is an act of worship. It becomes the heart-beat of a Christian's faith. In talking to God in prayer we offer praise and thanksgiving, we request forgiveness and, in general, make known our needs to Him.

We must learn patience. We must learn to wait upon the Lord. We cannot dictate to God as to how and when our prayers should be answered. God answers all proper prayers made in faith as Jesus tells us in Matthew 21:22, "All things whatsoever ye shall ask in prayer, believing, ye shall receive."

We must never try to hurry the decisions of God, only request that His will, not ours, be done. When we pray we must come before God in faith, with humbleness, with submission and with a willingness for His will to be done. Isaiah 57:15 tells us that God will dwell with him that is of a contrite and humble spirit.

Where hope is great, disappointment will be the more intense. Yet when frustration occurs, disheartening and disruptive as it may be, faith must not be weakened. Impatience and exasperation must never rule when an immediate answer to our prayers is not forthcoming.

While God answers every proper prayer made in faith in accordance with His promises, His answer may not always be in accord with our will. The apostle Paul speaks of such a situation in II Corinthians 12:8,9 where he writes, "For this thing I besought the Lord thrice, that it might depart from me. And he said unto me, My grace is sufficient for thee: for my strength is made perfect in weakness." Thus knowing what is best for us, God's answer to our prayer may be "no."

Prayers which are not made in faith and which are not in accordance with God's promises, including prayers for foolish or hurtful things, are in vain and will remain unanswered.

Prayers must be made in faith and with expectation. In Mark 11:24, Jesus says, "What things soever ye desire, when ye pray, believe that ye receive them, and ye shall have them." On the other hand, in James 4:3, we are told "Ye ask, and receive not, because ye ask amiss." Only God in His wisdom and knowledge knows what may be best for us.

The truly thankful Christian can always find a reason for gratitude to God, and the time to express this feeling of gratitude in prayer. When we pray we are in communion with God. Devotedly, we must place ourselves into His service. When our courage weakens, we can go to God in prayer for strength. We have His promise: "Lo, I am with you alway, even unto the end of the world." (Matthew 28:20).

## *How to Pray*

If prayer is made with confidence,
With hopeful expectation;
If made with love and gratitude
And not from desperation,
Then it will reach God's given space
And every single word,
Each plainly-spoken syllable
Shall certainly be heard.

But if prayer is merely said
In endless repetition
And filled with greedy, selfish wants
Or is a vain petition,
Then better it remain unsaid;
It will not reach God's throne.
The words will scatter with the wind,
Be lost, remain unknown.

## *Prayer for Strength*

God, give me strength to climb the hill,
To scale the topmost peak;
I need Thy help, Thy aid, Thy will,
My own is far too weak.

I care not if the road be rough
And rugged to my feet,
If Thou are near, that is enough —
My footsteps will be fleet.

## *A Father's Prayer*

Lord, make him rugged,
Make him firm and strong,
Sound of limb;
Give him a healthy mind.

Give him good reasoning. Let him stand
Impervious to calm or storm,
Serene, seeking no favor, standing firm, alone,
Staunch and secure against the stress of life.

Let him be just and merciful,
Know tenderness,
And teach him to be kind
But never soft or weak.

Make him courageous; let him fight the fight
Of the oppressed, the weak, the helpless ones;
Let prejudice and malice, hate and scorn,
Remain unknown to him.

May he know peace, humility. But if there be
The need to know deep grief, adversity,
May he not be embittered; may he know
Thy chastening is only for his good.

And, Father, may he always do Thy will.
Protect and guard him through each passing day.
Let Thy sweet love encompass him always.
My son! *Our* son!

## *God Answers Prayer*

God gives to us His holy Word
And tells us that our prayers are heard.

And when we ask for what we seek,
He hears before we even speak.

And when the things we think we need
Have substitutes, we must take heed.

Faith must not weaken nor grow dim;
We must not question why of Him.

Just leave our prayers with Him alone;
His mind is wiser than our own!

## *Prayer for New Living*

Lord, clear our minds of prejudice,
Intolerance and hate,
Let us be friends to one and all
And never irritate
Another soul by what we do
Or anything we say,
And give us hearts for friendliness
Throughout each passing day.

We only have a little while
To garner happiness,
The time is lessened every day
In which to do our best.
Give everyone a heart for love
And let each person send
Bright rays of friendship out — to go
From friend to friend to friend.

*Names of The Lord*

Wonderful,
profoundly significant
Are the names of the Lord.
Simple,
Eloquently fitting and appropriate,
Each is descriptive
Of His character,
His mission,
And His promise.

God called Him "My beloved Son."
Also "The Stone" upon which His house was built.
Jesus describes Himself as being
The "Way," the "Truth" and the "Life."

Timothy characterizes Him as being the
"Mediator" between God and men.
"Lamb of God" — means the sacrifice offered for all.
"Emmanuel" — God is with us.
"Messiah" — the expected king and deliverer.
"Bread of Life" — the wonderful provision that
God has made in Christ for the spiritual
needs of men.

"Redeemer" — the ransom paid by the atoning
blood of the Lamb.
"Prince of Peace" — the blessed fruit of peace
and of His wonderful kingdom to come.
"Christ" — the anointed one.

And "Jesus" — sweetest, simplest, the most
commonly-known, means our Saviour.

# Christian Living

"... walk humbly with thy God."

Micah 6:8

# Christian Living 

A three-fold pattern of conduct which is pleasing to God, is composed of justice, mercy and humility. These three virtues — for virtues they certainly are — are those things which will make a life consistently joyous.

The principles of morality and uprightness do not change nor vary. We can understand the standard of divine justice by only one phrase: "To do justly," for this is in conformity with God's revealed will.

To be merciful or to love mercy implies that we know and are saved by God's mercy. We are able to be merciful only because God is merciful to us.

The mark of Christian discipleship is "To walk humbly with God." The way to spiritual greatness is the way of humility. Our Lord has told us that "Whosoever humbleth himself shall be exalted." He has also told us "To do justly and to love mercy and to walk humbly with God."

We, as Christians, are called to be different, non-conformists to the world's way, especially when it comes to moral questions. We are to be transformed by our faith in Christ according to the patterns He established. Attempts of the world to appeal to lust and pride, things geared to the baser nature and the sensual appetites of men, are varied and many. Some of them are even hard to recognize as such.

The evil of sin is concealing, for it can darken our view of things so that we may forget the dangers. Sin can so engulf us that we lose sight of God, unless we guard ourselves against it. May we ever be mindful of the darkness of sin and evil and always seek for that light which will guide us on to life eternal!

The Bible is all-sufficient for our needs. We are told in 2 Timothy 3:16-17 that "All scripture is given by inspiration of God, and is profitable for doctrine, for reproof, for correction, for instruction in righteousness: that the man of God may be perfect, thoroughly furnished unto all good works."

Jesus states in John 8:12: "I am the light of the world: he that followeth me shall not walk in darkness, but shall have the light of life."

Living a Christian life means living a Christ-like life. Paul states in Galatians 2:20 "I live; yet not I, but Christ liveth in me."

We, therefore, have a responsibility to God's law, namely, obedience. This is not a privilege, it is a command given by God. We may live a life of fruitfulness only if we abide in Him, following His commands and teachings and letting Him lead us with His blessed light.

## *Rebuke*

I sat beside my opened door,
Ready to welcome Him.
The other ragged passersby, —
The lame with vision dim,
The weak, the weary, hungry ones, —
They passed without my aid;
I could not risk to take the time
To help them — so afraid.

That He might come and pass my door
And fail to recognize
My dwelling place. The day grew late.
Then, suddenly, my eyes
Beheld Him standing there! My joy
Complete, I welcomed: "Lord,
Please enter in my humble home.
Your place has been prepared.

"I waited long for You to come!"
He smiled and gently said:
"I passed by many times, my son;
Each time, you turned your head."

## *A Happy Life*

Thrice happy am I in His love
And this to Him I owe;
I love Him, and my friend in Him,
And, for His sake, my foe.

## *Togetherness*

Dark silhouettes atop the hill —
The father and the son
Stand side by side, as good men will,
As they have always done.

They view their acres far below
With eyes of joy and pride.
The father feels an inner glow,
His loved son by his side.

The son, no less than father, feels
A fullness of the heart.
Togetherness then gently seals;
All other things depart.

## *Before Sleep Comes*

Each night, before I go to sleep,
I like to think that I have done
A deed of kindness, given aid
Or courage to someone afraid,
Before the setting of the sun.

I like to think that someone else
Was helped by me, that I was there
When they were friendless and in need,
And that by my small, simple deed,
They knew that someone else could care.

I like to feel that He, above,
Looks down with favor, with a smile.
And knows how hard I try each day
To walk the narrow Christian way,
And walks beside me all the while.

## *Patterned Ways*

I shall walk in my father's steps,
Not because it is easy,
But because I like the deep marks
He always makes. They are easy to follow,
Whether I trudge behind him in the snow,
Through high tall grasses, along the dunes,
Or follow him through his ploughed furrows.

When I was small, I had to stretch
My legs to match his stride.
Sometimes I failed,
But *always* I tried.

He shows no sign — nor has he ever shown a sign —
He is aware of this, my following;
He sets his patterned mark for me
And, filled with pride, I bravely follow him.

Now, having grown a bit, I tread behind
With ease. Occasionally, (unless I watch myself),
I walk with even longer stride
And over-reach his tracks,
Make new ones of my own.

God, grant that I shall make a patterned way
As clear for my own son!

*Legacy for My Son*

Lean purse I leave you,
　　Though without regret,
You'll find that money
　　Is not that hard to get.
But other things
　　I have to leave to you:
The grass and hills,
　　The stars, the sky so blue,
The meadows, streams,
　　The seasons as they come;
Your journeying
　　Can be a joyous sum.

I leave you dreams,
　　A sense of right and wrong,
A thankful heart
　　And in that heart a song;
I leave you friends,
　　A gift for making more;
I leave you time —
　　My son, there's much in store
For you to see,
　　To know, to hear, to do.
All precious things
　　Are those I leave to you!

### *Vulnerable*

A man may build about his heart
A breastplate made of finest steel
And proudly boast he cannot feel
The pain of any blow or dart.

Unless his heart is free of sin,
His great security is vain;
His armor shall be cleaved in twain
If evil purpose works within.

### *Humility*

He that is down need have no fear of falling;
He that is low has neither shame nor pride.
But he that walks with humbleness of spirit
Knows deeply that he has God for a guide.

And even though he walks with heavy burden
And knows the way is rugged and is far,
He still can have the inward strength and courage
To keep his eyes forever on a star.

### *God's Chosen Way*

Who lives a life of selfishness,
In greed with thoughts debased,
Who's bigoted or filled with hate,
Will live a life of waste.

But he who lives unselfishly,
Does good from day to day,
Will live a rich, full life, for he
Lives God's own chosen way.